J569.7
A1. 93

D0743139

J 569.7
Oliver, Rupert.
Woolly rhinoceros.

Ice-Age Monsters

Woolly Rhinoceros

Written by Rupert Oliver
Illustrated by Andrew Howat

Library of Congress Cataloging in Publication Data

Oliver, Rupert.
    Woolly rhinoceros.

    (Ice age monsters)
    Summary: Follows a woolly rhinoceros through her
day as she encounters many other inhabitants of her
prehistoric world.
    1. Woolly rhinoceros—Juvenile literature.
2. Paleontology—Pleistocene—Juvenile literature.
[1. Woolly rhinoceros.   2. Rhinoceros.   3. Mammals,
Fossil.   4. Prehistoric animals]   I. Title.   II. Series:
Oliver, Rupert.   Ice age monsters.
QE882.U6068   1986   569'.7   86-3955
ISBN 0-86592-848-7

Rourke Enterprises, Inc.
Vero Beach, FL 32964

Megaceros

Saber Tooth Tiger

Cave Bear

Ice-Age Monsters
Woolly Rhinoceros

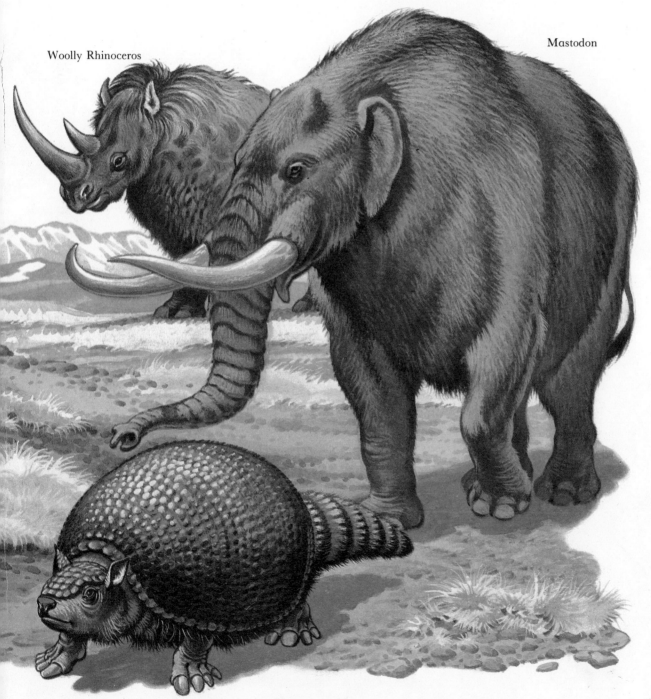

Woolly Rhinoceros

Mastodon

Glyptodon

Woolly Rhinoceros plodded through the patch of snow. Not far away was a piece of open land where the grass was beginning to grow. There would be some good food there. Close by, a small herd of Woolly Mammoths were feeding. They were sweeping their tusks to and fro in the snow, pushing it aside to reach the plants underneath.

In recent days the weather had been getting
warmer. The snow, which had covered the whole
land, had melted until only patches remained.
Perhaps Spring was coming and Woolly Rhinoceros
would have to move North to avoid the hot weather
which was so uncomfortable.

Woolly Rhinoceros suddenly stopped in her tracks. She had seen something moving. There, in the bushes, it moved again. At first Woolly Rhinoceros could not make out what it was. It was covered with fur, but it did not smell or move like any animal she had seen before. Then, something else moved in the bushes and Woolly Rhinoceros realized what was hiding. It was man. There seemed to be quite a few of them, though they remained hidden.

Woolly Rhinoceros knew that man could be very dangerous. Man was one of the most skilled hunters in the world. Woolly Rhinoceros began to back off, keeping her head down and her horn pointed toward the men.

The men did not seem to be very interested in Woolly Rhinoceros. They were paying more attention to the small herd of Woolly Mammoths. The Mammoths were slowly moving closer to the clump of bushes where the men were hiding.

One of the Woolly Mammoths moved close to the bushes. Suddenly a spear flew out from the bushes and buried itself in the side of the Mammoth. The animal roared in pain and turned to run away. Before it could move far, however, the men had sprung from cover and plunged even more spears and some axes into the creature. It was over in seconds and the Mammoth lay dead on the ground. Its roar had alerted the other Woolly Mammoths which quickly moved off. Woolly Rhinoceros, too, moved away from the men and their weapons.

Nearby was the sound of a splashing river. Spring must certainly be coming if the waters were melting. Woolly Rhinoceros walked down to the river to drink. As she approached the river bank Woolly Rhinoceros realized that she was not alone.

Peering intently into the waters was a Cave Bear. Suddenly the claw of the Cave Bear lashed down into the river and a fish flipped out on to the bank. The Cave Bear had her young with her and she allowed them to eat the fish. As the Woolly Rhinoceros approached, the Cave Bear looked up. She had nothing to fear from Woolly Rhinoceros, so the Cave Bear went back to fishing.

Having drunk her fill, Woolly Rhinoceros
climbed away from the river. On the open tundra the
plants were starting to grow again after the long
Winter. Grazing on the sparse grass was a large
Megaceros. Close by was a small herd of Musk
Oxen. Woolly Rhinoceros could smell the Musk
Oxen before she could see them because they gave off
a very powerful odor.

The Megaceros raised its head at a slight noise. Woolly Rhinoceros had heard it too and looked in the direction from which it came. Megaceros ran past Woolly Rhinoceros, calling out alarm. Woolly Rhinoceros could not see anything. Megaceros must have had better eyesight than Woolly Rhinoceros.

One of the Musk Oxen gave a cry of fear and the small herd began to bunch together. The young Musk Oxen stayed on the inside of the group while the adults stood around them. Across the tundra came trotting a pack of wolves. The adult Musk Oxen lowered their heads and presented their horns to the wolves.

The wolves did not even stop, nor did they try to attack the Musk Oxen. Instead, the wolves ran on across the plain, passing the plant eaters in peace. Perhaps they had smelled the blood of the Mammoth the men had killed. Wolves could usually pick up some scraps of food from such a kill.

The Musk Oxen spread out again into the loose formation. Woolly Rhinoceros started to graze on the meager plants which grew on the ground. There were some tasty, succulent shoots here, but most of the food was coarse growth from last year. It would be some time yet before there would be enough fresh food for Woolly Rhinoceros to eat. All through the Winter she had lived off the fat she had stored up the Summer before. Now almost all the fat had been used and Woolly Rhinoceros was very hungry indeed.

Far to the West ominous clouds were banking up. Woolly Rhinoceros was too busy eating to notice them or to realize what they meant.

As Woolly Rhinoceros grazed she gradually moved away from the Musk Oxen. Soon she was all alone on the open tundra. The dark clouds were even closer now and, at last, Woolly Rhinoceros noticed that they were there. She sniffed the air and felt that a change in the weather was on the way.

Then Woolly Rhinoceros smelled something else. She had smelled that particular odor once before and knew that it meant danger. Loping across the grass, passing between the bushes was a Homotherium. Woolly Rhinoceros knew how sharp were the fangs of a Homotherium. She lowered her head toward the cat. The Homotherium spotted Woolly Rhinoceros and moved forward to attack. Woolly Rhinoceros knew that her best chance was to attack as well. She charged forward with her horn pointing upwards, hoping to hit the Homotherium.

She missed, but her charge had frightened the Homotherium. Woolly Rhinoceros turned and faced the Homotherium. The cat was getting ready to pounce. Woolly Rhinoceros charged again. Once more the Homotherium had to get out of the way.

Woolly Rhinoceros was now getting tired. She could not charge many more times and when she stopped charging the Homotherium would be able to attack her. It was then that the dark clouds passed overhead and the last blizzard of the Winter struck. The wind whipped past the two animals and the snow fell down in a solid curtain. The Homotherium disappeared in the snow and Woolly Rhinoceros was able to escape in safety.

The Woolly Rhinoceros and the Pleistocene Ice Ages

Pleistocene Europe, showing the maximum extent of the ice sheets

The time of ice and snow

Life has existed on this planet for hundreds of millions of years, but it is only during the past 60 million years that mammals have been important. Scientists have named this era the Cainozoic, which means recent life, and have divided it into a number of periods. The most recent of these periods is known as the Pleistocene which began two million years ago. During the course of the Pleistocene the climate of the world had undergone sudden and dramatic changes. Before that time the climate of the earth remained fairly constant over millions of years. But during the Pleistocene it suddenly became much colder. Great rivers of ice, called glaciers, crept down from the mountains and the polar ice caps spread out to cover far more land than they do today. Even where there were no glaciers and ice caps, the weather became much colder than it had been before. After several thousand years the weather grew warmer again. Then, after another long interval, the glaciers began

to advance once more. This happened several times during the Pleistocene and scientists still do not agree as to why this happened.

Lifestyle of the Woolly Rhinoceros

The Woolly Rhinoceros was specially adapted to the cold conditions of the Pleistocene ice ages. The intensely cold climate meant that much of Europe was stripped of its normal vegetation and tundra spread across the continent. Tundra is the name given to the type of landscape seen in this book. For much of the year the land lay under snow, but during the short Summer, plants grew with amazing speed and vitality. Even so, it was too cold for trees or any other large plant to survive and the tundra is generally flat and monotonous. Landscapes of this kind can be found in northern Canada and Russia today. The Woolly Rhinoceros had many special adaptations to help it survive in such inhospitable conditions. Most noticeable was its shaggy coat which gave it its name. The reddish-brown fur was in two layers to help it keep out the cold. There was a layer of strong, thick hair which was a protection against the bitter wind, even in the depths of Winter. Beneath this was a layer of short, soft fur which was capable of retaining the body warmth of the animal very efficiently. With a total length of just ten feet, the Woolly Rhinoceros was smaller than its ancestors. This meant that it needed less food to survive in the food-scarce tundra. It was also able to store vast reserves of fat under its skin. During the short Summer the Woolly Rhinoceros would eat as much as possible to build up its fat. When Winter brought food shortages the animal could then survive on its fat supply.

Animals of the ice ages

All the animals in the story lived at the same time and in the same place. The Woolly Mammoth is perhaps the best known of these. Like the Woolly Rhinoceros, the Mammoth was a type of animal adapted to a cold climate, though most other Mammoths lived in warmer areas. It had the same two layers of fur as the Woolly Rhinoceros and was also smaller than others of its kind. It is thought that the Mammoth used its tusks to brush aside snow so that it could reach food on the ground. The Megaceros is also known as the Irish Elk, because a lot of its bones have been found in Ireland. It was a

gigantic species of deer which had the largest antlers ever to grow on a deer. One set of antlers has been found measuring 12 feet across. The Cave Bear gained its name because scientists found so many of the animals bones in caves. It is believed that Cave Bears hibernated during the long cold Winter, just as modern bears do, and that some died in their dens during the Winter. The Homotherium was the last in a long line of spectacular animals. It was a type of Saber Tooth Cat which somehow managed to survive for thousands of years after the other species became extinct. All these now extinct animals seem to have died out as the last ice age came to a close. Some scientists think this was due to the arrival of warmer weather to which the creatures were not adjusted. Others believe that the spread of man had a lot to do with extinction. Groups of men hunted most of the large plant eating animals so they may have been hunted to extinction, as almost happened to the American Bison last century. Of all the animals in the story only the Musk Oxen and the wolves still survive. Musk Oxen live in Greenland and northern Canada where tundra still exists, but they were very rare. Wolves were common in most temperate regions until a few hundred years ago. They now survive in remote areas. Man is undoubtedly the most numerous of all the creatures in our story. He has not only survived but thrived.

The adaptations of the Woolly Rhinoceros to a cold climate.

Height: 4½ feet
Length: 10 feet

Thick fur to keep warm

Strong horn for defense

Small size requires less food

Layers of fat to store food